Praise for *Without a Field Guide*

The poems in *Without a Field Guide* are elegant, understated, finely wrought. Nicole Robinson explores trauma with a stunningly deft touch and enormous heart. She has a keen eye for the living world and speaks truth with complexity and compassion. Robinson writes, "Like Whitman, she thinks / she'll do nothing for a while but listen." This beautiful debut collection shows what such deep listening can reveal."

Ellen Bass, Author of *Indigo*

There is a spine of light which runs through this book, though the poems quite often diverge from one another, from the delicate landscapes of our threatened natural world to the poet's inner life, growing up female and lesbian, "straddling centuries" in America. It's been a pleasure to greet this fine and long-awaited first collection.

Dorianne Laux, Author of *Only as the Day is Long*

In the tradition of Wordsworth and Rachel Carson, Whitman and Mary Oliver, these poems sing of the natural world, its balance and healing, its roots and leaves, its magnificent great blue heron. I admire their images, "field notes," interwoven with an inner landscape that runs the gamut from shame and regret to beauty and love. I admire their grounded honesty and the sane humility of their voice.

Joseph Millar, Author of *Dark Harvest: New and Selected Poems*

When we are lost, stitched shut, when are struck, what "leads the heart back," I see, are bones, potatoes, beans, wings in the freezer, the quivering leaf-flags ants carry up the trunk of a tree. Or no, what leads the heart back is the singing of. Robinson's voice breaks what's frozen into an opening. No guide perhaps, but singing all around. "I held my hand and stood up." Indeed.

Kate Northrop, Author of *Homewrecker*

I have such deep affection for these poems, which follow and lead and rend and comfort and guide me, which love me — yes! these poems love me, as I wander their landscapes of blessed damage, and my own. Here, water is "a god who punches the shore in the center / of our chest, leaves a gasp of breath / to name the moment when the inhale / isn't enough," the deer learn to survive by shopping at Dick's Sporting Goods, and tenderness comes to us, clutches us, until we sing. This is a book that never flinches from grief, while also helping us glimpse raw, wild, sometimes even raucous redemption everywhere we look.

Ruth L. Schwartz, Author of *Miraculum*

Without a
Field Guide

Without a
Field Guide Nicole
Robinson

UNBOUND EDITION PRESS

Atlanta

FIRST EDITION

Printed in the United States of America

LIBRARY OF CONGRESS RECORD

Name: Robinson, Nicole, 1981– author.
Title: Without a Field Guide / Nicole Robinson.
Edition: First edition.
Published: Atlanta : Unbound Edition Press, 2023.

LCCN: 2022951806
LCCN Permalink: https://lccn.loc.gov/2022951806
ISBN: 978-0-9913780-9-8 (hardcover)

Designed by Eleanor Safe and Joseph Floresca
Printed by Bookmobile, Minneapolis, MN
Distributed by Small Press Distribution

123456789

Unbound Edition Press
1270 Caroline Street, Suite D120
Box 448
Atlanta, GA 30307

for Deb

Contents

III

Without a Field Guide

I

Straddling Centuries

I only lived in the twentieth century for twenty years
but between the mixtapes and dial-up

the girl I was got stuck in a hush on her bed,
all bone sore from the world's heat,

its reactionary blisters. She's alone and unable to fade.
Too wise to leave, too sad to stay, she tried to get off

what she couldn't get back: her small body
like a thin summer dress. I'd call to her

if I could, from cell towers, through phone lines
tell her, *leave home and not the body you'll need.*

Genesis I

Something about the goat's rectangular pupil
pulls me closer each time I bend to pet the wiry
hair of his neck. Something about
the way I reach out, the way he so plainly refuses.

Body of the Great Blue Heron

Body of the great blue heron, mostly grey, body of morning,
body to hold the torrent of water and still land,

body with gravity and flight, and who doesn't love
a contradiction? Body of neck, length of a snake, body

with a dagger for a bill and barrel for torso. What do we hold
in our chests? Blood and an exhale we can't let go, memory

and muscle, a whole body of breath. Heron's got a body
of hollow bones. What lives inside that space?

Is that where the soul lives, in whatever cavity
it can find? Is that our soul when we're alone that thuds

in our chest against the breastbone? Heron's body of feather
and fringed claw is a body beside a colony of bodies

who prefers to forage alone. Body of freshwater,
body of salt, body with legs disappearing underwater.

The heron will defend its feeding territory:
throw its wings open, tilt its head back,

point its bill toward sky, and stretch itself
as large as it can, a body of belief. It will lift

with one flap of its wings, carry its body through the body of sky.

Voice

There you were and there you vanished
until a spine of silence snapped
like something I heard before I understood.
What sounds will you stutter into light?
When will I accept you as mine?
I watch primrose petals press against the sepal,
reveal stamen and pistil, too tender for daylight.
It opens and I look for you
to say what needs said. But you're silent.
An opossum climbs out of a hole from under the porch.
"Hello," I whisper. The opossum crosses the street
and disappears without a sound.

Because of Beatitude

A bird can only fly so long after injury
from a mower. Once tight-beaked in a camouflage

of weeds, now it flies for everyone to see —
flawlessly with its yellow chest and white patch

at the back of its wings — until
it tries to land but fumbles upward

again, and we see its legs are gone, little stubs of pink.
Can you imagine the yellow rail's final landing?

Does the bird fly as high as it can just to quit
and plunge to the ground? Or does it die there —

in air — one last trusting beat of its wings?
Of course, the death of the bird isn't the point.

The point has to be the bird's life: what it saw,
and who saw it while flying so blessedly damaged.

Genesis II

She places her terrarium locket around my neck
and tells me the plants can survive inside
with only a bit of mulch. I admire the fence
she built, the starred sky. The moss she sculpted as trees
looked large as oaks. The locket is so light
I can hardly feel its weight — except, this:
the habitat that lives tucked behind glass
has one small man peering over the fence.
If I knew how to open it, I would remove him.

The Body Keeps the Score

This is my body: here a cell, there a cell,
an immune system ready

to pounce without threat. By accident
it attacks itself. Cells against cells.

Strange disease? Autobiography,
please? Not now, I can't breathe.

Autoimmune disease, automatic
distraction, abstract idiopathic

anaphylaxis, or just under the weather
when the weather was under

my skin, a thunderstorm within.
We all go hiding from ourselves

sometimes. What we find needs found.

Where Nothing

I saw a gull struck
by a red truck
and it looked like a piñata
bursting, flanking
in air, where nothing
but the lick
of a windshield wiper
smeared a silent prayer
for the white
feathers flittering.

Elegy

for Christian O'Keeffe 1991 — 2012

Squirrels are surviving, leaping from wires
while cell towers connect us —
and your cat in the house
lives slowly in a world
with windows and walls to keep it safe.

You said the world was splicing
and spinning ethers, it didn't matter,
said inside the sun of your closed eyes
life was still as a statue —
but I have never known one so still, until
I picked up the phone to dial your number
then remembered you were dead.

And now autumn is crawling
into winter. First, it drops what it holds
then stares at the sky, like you must have done
on the tracks that night. The trees
looked like the steps of a strange castle,
one branch closer to God.

Opossum

Once the maggots nibbled on its split belly
it looked like it was breathing again.
Life swarmed in. The opossum
was out of its fur: muscles brown,
picked over, uncovered. Vultures came
to claim what they could:
ribs as clean as wires, eyes no longer there
to show a reflection. Just empty sockets,
just bones stock-piled
beside fur, just a bit of muscle
waiting to be taken by larva lingering.
How strange when they grow dark,
seemingly dead, until
they break out of themselves and fly.

At the Black Swamp Bird Observatory
Banding Station

Warblers squirm silent when caught in mist nets
then peck at the hands of the ornithologist
who says, "We shortchange the migration tale."
He means we leave out the struggle: lack
of stopover habitat, windmills, buildings,
jaws of a housecat, and only a small percent of birds
arrive on breeding grounds. And what of our own

migrations? The boxes stacked by walls,
smell of cardboard and sweat, the emptied desk,
our bodies that remind us they're our only home.
How lonely we are inside them. How little
we know of them — moments
we look in a mirror as if to study a stranger.

At the Black Swamp Bird Observatory among the leaf-out
of trees, that green, the marsh pressed
against Lake Erie, the ornithologist bands and releases
a blackpoll warbler to the clean back of morning.
It lifts the sky to join a winged stampede
on a journey toward its next temporary home
while we save what we can
of the marsh, of our own tired bodies.

Dear Great Blue Heron

Nothing scares you. Nothing
blinks your wings

to flight. I watch you
build a statue

of yourself
on the riverbank.

I tell you the currents
I crave, how I've hollowed

love out of loving
and am always finding feathers

to fan the days away,
to pluck the pain

before I know the bones
of its fingers, like his

fingers, sanding
the edges of my life.

Without a Field Guide

This is where I learned to let go: here
where the house finch calls for unknown
reasons, where the starling picks the suet
no matter what season shatters
above it, where all the birds bounce their sheen
against sky also worthy of my stopping.
Without an equation, without longing to burst
into meaning, I loosen life with the boughs
of a dogwood whose flowers are mouths
opening. I am as human as the mother
who birthed me, who left me
a story where I featherstitch wings
to a page without a field guide to identify
who I am or where I'm flying.

Genesis III

The jellyfish, clear but filmed in its slime,
is dead on the shore, wordless as always.
I'm stupidly in love with the story
I'll never know of its life. I turn it over
with a stick, careful not to deflate it.

What the Bones Say

Our language, a series of single notes, cracks
a different rhythm each time. We touch

and don't feel. Never the same song twice.
Never a bone with a twin voice.

Believer of muscle and strength,
we may not live like organs pulsing,

but we structure shadows, break without bend.
Who, if not we, will carry your history?

II

To Clarify

I mean to say those deer walked
into Dick's Sporting Goods

to buy their own camouflage —
I mean the girl I was at ten

keeps hiding, and the one at nineteen,
I never met — I mean they keep

trying to smell the iris
and wear its pollen

for make-up — I mean
they got lost like any coin tossed

into a wish, the way ice
on Lake Erie disappears

into itself — I mean those deer
only wanted to go shopping

to find some way to survive.

Where the goldfinch

sits at the thistle feed and shudders
her call toward branches of trees,

all bone against bone, alive as summer,
though green's long gone to winter,

I'm sixteen in the hot tub on the patio.
He says, "Move closer to the jets,"

and stutters on about God's gifts
while I study that goldfinch's call,

learn to match the rhythm,
to no longer long, to leave the body

and fly to the branches, sing so quietly
the song fades instead of crashes.

Secret

What if this secret has legs?
What if the legs are mine?

What if I tell you flowers
arranged in the hallway
with dusty yellow heads
pretend to be tulips and wear
fingerprints like labyrinths?

What if this secret learns
to walk? How long will she travel
the center of my thumbprint
before sliding inside the petals?

What if she walks back out?

When the secret says,
"I loved him — he loved
my breasts, and I let him
because my heart was hungry
and hiding behind them — "
what of her voice is mine?

Shame

I grew you, fine
as a suit of skin
meant to last decades,
poly thread to match
the fabric
so no one can see
how you're held
together. Look at you
looking like me.
I pinned the parts
to take in. Stitch by stitch
from fitting to finish,
I learned your posture
and we postured
as one. The garment
took time, but after
the precision
of perfection, the cuff point
and the drape, the hidden
pockets where we keep
those solid secrets,
it's hard to take off.

Loneliness

Ash of pinon incense, lamps
unlit, fan unplugged, the heart

spent, space hollow enough to hold
anything. But what comes is an echo

you can't understand. Somewhere:
laughter, wine glasses clinking,

bicycle tires on gravel, your friend's voice
before the breakdown. Whatever you don't hear

behind the rattle and rush of thoughts
is stuck in a city where the voice travels

when it has no words to write and mail.
Loneliness knows you'll keep reaching

your hand into your empty mailbox.

PTSD

Pre-trauma? Strong dreams before
I remember — or an almost memory:

an evergreen tree, blue sky, blur of words
smashed with berries between fingers. Ordinary

snapped before it grew. Distance was forced
between the pieces of me, whole gorges

gouged in the psyche. I censored
sorrow, hid inside smiles to absorb

my life like a game, a sport
where I listed what I saw and heard: car horn,

oak tree, streetlight, roach by the door,
goatee, bobwhite, trash on the floor,

a postcard never sent. I tried armor
but there were cracks. Now, I reroute

brain channels like detours to create
a strange order, stay alive, anchor.

Genesis IV

I curled into his arms

like the smallest branches tucked
in overgrown grass.

like graffiti written quietly
underneath the overpass
where you could see
JT loved LM since '93
only if you were looking for it.

like cherry blossom petals bent
into mulch after rain.

because they were open.

Self-portrait in Fragments

bluff of bone,
nest of hair,
breath from the buzz of bees —

forest of scars,
drainpipe throat,
manic mess of puberty —

bronzed bruise,
banged-up fists,
red roads on maps of eyes —

hinge of mouth,
muscle of maker,
soul unseen, split —

My Shadow

My shadow's rarely seen in Ohio's winter,
too grey and dim for reflection. All night

it cradles me through dreams
I can't remember. *Here's a part of me,*

it wants to say on a morning
when the sun yawns. I spin

and it hardly moves before
it disappears. *Tell me what happened*

last night in the dark under dark,
I beg. It can't whisper in the void

of itself. It exists in nothing.

At the Churchyard

It was a marsh where mosquitoes never masked their longing
for mud, or the blood of anyone. He arrived early

to listen to songbirds, to watch how they rested
on brambles to sing what only they knew

they were singing. If we could learn the leaning of their language
we wouldn't have so many questions, would we?

He moved his hands across her body like a hot evening,
a kind of calling that steamed. Sometimes night slid

so gently over the horizon she forgot
it was swallowing the day.

Honored After Failed Rescue

The lifeguard found the man facedown behind rocks
and six-foot waves at the Fingal Spit
when the bronze fist of the sun lifted over
the Tasman Sea. Some call the spit a deathtrap,
a rattle back, an almost sand-bridge to the island.

Believe the body the surfer thought as he paddled
over waves before he drowned. The lifeguard dove
to pull the surfer to shore — then, CPR
all reckless: like twigs the ribs went snapping.

Hero of the sea, hero of pulling a dead body to shore
and not dying himself, the lifeguard received an award
for trying. Tides tumbled in, sand shrank back,
and the surfer's mother gripped a photo
of her son as a child building castles on the beach.
Her thumb had rubbed the ink from his face.

To the Poet, from the Poem

Your body is a small town, and honey,
this is a shakedown. All shame and secrets
tucked in pockets with torn tissues, I will find them
and make you say what he said: "If you had a father
you would know this is what they do."

And stop marking the margins
with, *don't use this word*. Just write it.
All words stretch themselves then travel
to the edge. They catch in the town hall
meeting of your head where ten years ago
I called and called, pulled caps off pens,
then you stopped me, left the blank page hungry.

But today this town restructures: the pen
in your hand, the ink of your voice is mine.

Letter to Shame

You staple sound to language — even a compliment drowns
in the haze of you, crawls in with good intentions

and is covered in stench: some Allegheny songbird
lingering in a landfill. You learn the chord of C

to stay in the middle, reminding me who taught me
to sing, to tilt my head so many ways. At night

you won't let me sleep. You hum the price of the Lord's prayer
I can't afford to believe. You think I love you,

love the fog you cover me in, and I do.
I can hide everyone inside you.

Inside, only you know I hate myself so beautifully.
Remember how I started to pull you out of me?

Holes appeared. People crawled out and the holes opened
into trails. Remember the last time I led a hike

with kids in Ohio? A little girl asked
if we'd see elephants in the woods. When I said, "No — "

she asked if we could go deeper in and find them.

Foster Family

He lifted his voice from Saturday night's
whispers, then twisted a congregation
to tears during Sunday's praise. He taught me
how to dip bread in wine until I was bloody
and broken, one with Jesus. He was the minister
of music and I the usher of nothing.

The mother was thin, high-octane
and bricked as the Berlin Wall:
half of an iron curtain I couldn't break through.
She sang back-up, a voice so soprano
she silenced rooms. I choked on words, turned blue.

He sank songs into baptisms, fondled notes,
tipped the tune into hearts. He lifted one hand
to the Lord and the other played the piano.

To be close to God I carried a Bible
with pages wrinkled, words too worn
to be read. On Saturday night I pretended
to hold God, those notes, that praise
until it felt close to the smell
of cinnamon rolls cooling on Sunday's counter
where I hummed her high notes, his low strokes,
and a story I learned not to sing.

Boneyard Beach
Jacksonville, Florida

A gull calls and disappears into fog at Boneyard Beach
where trees uprooted from erosion reach their bone-white branches

like hands toward the Atlantic. What will I reach for
when I die? The ice melt in the Arctic raises sea-levels

thousands of miles away and waves crash to this shore.
Is there ever distance between us? There's a girl here

who leaps over sea foam and ducks under tree bones. She taps a tree —
"You're it!" she screams, then laughs, skips further into fog, further

from me. I wave but she doesn't see. I climb the fallen tree
she tapped like it was a whale I'd ride in her game of tag

at sea. This nothing around us could be something that saves us.
Fog thickens in front of the tree while its roots behind me

stay rooted to air. The girl is gone from what I can see. Under me
a dead gull lies in the sand pinning a green leaf.

Below

God you are more grit-gold than shine
and I am too burnt to be your bride.
Still, I love your curly answers: the evening
primrose knows when to open; those geese,
just past hatching, know to open their mouths
when hungry. I know when I needed a family:
autumn bobbed its young colors
and you coaxed me through. God, I wanted
to kill you. But I turned you into a wind-wish
answer, a swampland, a cry below
the honking of geese migrating.

Up from the Basement, from the Photos

Imagine a girl climbs up from the basement,
from the photos of ancestors on the wall, the lines
that connect her to mothers and grandmothers
and into mountains where she stretches new twig legs,
a neck that tilts tall and arms that turn blue
with feathers. She lifts as a heron, flies next to trees hoping
they will lead her to Whitman, and they do, or at least to a rock
where he might have perched. There she stares at the world
and knows the mother lost in her stories, sometimes
in her flames, the child who has to search
for a safe place to play, brown-headed cowbirds
dropping their eggs in other birds' nests, the man who loved
and hurt the girl he raised. There's a compass plant
lining up north and south and at the end of summer sprouts
long-stemmed yellow flowers. There's the baby she was
and a mother unable to hold her. Like Whitman, she thinks
she'll do nothing for a while but listen.

Genesis V

One night I said, *Hello, little one,*
friend inside my skin. I said it until
I believed it and walked to the pond
where I misheard a frog
as a birdcall. Then, silence
and dumb luck: cattails
swaying. I watched a frog leap
to water, watched the ripples ride over.

III

Genesis VI

I'm tucked so far in the mountain
I forget I'm on a mountain.
The trees are too close — I can't see the horizon.
I study the edges of myself against the edges
of trees and shrubs that line the gravel drive
I drove to arrive here, a trunk full
of yesterday's longings.
In secret, I unpacked them.
In secret, I studied their histories
then met their needs and set them free.
Who am I in this beginning?
A brown creeper spirals the trunk
of an oak, reaches the top
and clumsily drops like a leaf to the base
of the next tree. It starts its climb again.
Its camouflaged body could be mistaken for a knot
on a tree, but it can't stand still. It's too hungry.
My past is down the mountainside swallowed by fog
and it doesn't need me anymore. I stop looking
for an overlook, bend down, knees in the dirt
like prayer, watch an ant carry a leaf
across the trunk of a fallen tree, a green flag
waving me on saying, *go* —
though I don't know where.

The Truth About Love

after W.H. Auden

It could be the pine grosbeak flicking its notes
to sound like B.B. King, or the gaze of a child
standing in the sun staring at a still swing.

If you look inside your apartment and can't find it,
split the drywall open. You wouldn't be the first

to destroy for love. America waves it with a flag,
sends it to war. Sometimes it swells into sex, sometimes
it's layered like a storm shivering against shingles.

It will not stop when you want to be quiet.
It will stagger, sheaf, alter everything.

Wing in the Freezer

To understand desire be Angerona
in Rome, one finger over your mouth.

Her statue was found in a shrine
for the Goddess of Pleasure. By the way,

there's a wing in my freezer. It's April
and I'm in Ohio taking photos of snowdrops.

Snowdrops are early spring flowers,
small balloons of white hanging from leaves.

In my dream, I was Voluptas.
Good morning pleasure,

or — good morning, Pleasure. Angerona
lifted her finger from her lips

and told me a secret. I promised
to keep it, but I'll share this:

when desire and pleasure meet,
stars connect like the street lights I pass

when I drive to assist in the after-death migration
of birds: grass to freezer to natural history museum.

I forgot to tell you it's a blue-winged teal
wing pinned to cardboard,

and it's next to a flicker and finch
found dead in the grass by the road.

A hunter friend killed the teal in season, ate it,
then gave me the wing. I'm vegan,

but he knew I had a freezer of berries
and dead birds. The birds are for science.

The berries are for me. I don't feed the dead,
but last night I spoke with them.

Mardi Gras in the Bayou

Not gumbo, beads, and breasts, not hangovers
and folks stumbling home half-dressed —

there's the patched light in the trees, children on their knees
saying prayers. Who knows what sounds sink

in the swamp: the thwack of a switch
on a child's legs, children shouting "Pardon!"

while they speak their memorized prayers. The elders fear
their elders who fear and miss the days parents had horses

and whips — the days children couldn't escape.
I've known that sound. I've worn scriptures

around my neck. Some words would stick,
others crawled out of my mouth —

they died before they made it to God.

Landscape

"Land" and "scape." The first

— some pitch of earth, desert or green,
or an idiom like "land on your feet" —

always outweighs the last

— call it the fast way of saying escape,
but under all water: all land.

Split like that, the words drift

— stream like a blurred meaning:
tunnel vision watching TV —

strangely, but together they build

— a fishhook in the dried-up wash
by the blooming cactus barrel —

the description of some great travel

— the way we forget to love the mundane
until something jolts the day —

and we find our selves inside ourselves.

Girl on the Playground

There's a child on a swing not swinging —
others are empty and still, bent

from weight disappeared. The metal
slide behind her is faded at its center.

What is she looking at? Where are her friends?
The green field is patched with mud, traffic hums

all muffled. What leads the heart back to itself?
The creak of the swing when it starts

to move? Her small legs pushing the air,
her arms pulling her weight.

Fieldnotes in February at Dawn

What you hoped to find,
what you longed for
and couldn't let go:
pink and purple sunrise
over a frozen lake
where deer stand below
the scotch pines
highlighted by snow,
won't be here,
won't wake you
into wonder. Instead,
a cloud cover
low enough it greys
the tops of trees as dawn ends
and light begins to slide
onto the frozen landscape,
the way you opened yourself
to yourself until
you realized you arrived
where you didn't know
you needed to be
but knew it was right
because you could breathe.
Strange how change happens
so slowly you forget
you're noticing

the colors of green
against the white of snow,
the first chirps
of a dark-eyed junco.
Sign of waking life,
sign of singing
what you didn't know
you knew.

Hook & Life

Near tilt of the toy-top done spinning,
near nectar, ripened blackberries, near
never wanting to be undone, near crawling
after crying, near the child of me I was longing

to find, near nasty, near holy morning
cigarette, near notes marked in the margins
of a Bible or self-help manual, near
exhale of bubbles the girl made trying

to drown, near a pool sign reading: "Hook & Life
ring for emergency use only," near
a still frame past always present, near
acceptance, I held my hand and stood up.

The Privilege of Watching Neighborhood Baseball

Let's end the night with an image, a lean
on the wall by the window while children
in the field across the street play baseball
late evening in February. Everything's hotter

this year: our tempers, the climate, the fear
my student wears who wants to go home
to Afghanistan — but can't. There's the pang of pain
in my chest when I try to breathe. Call it the heart

choking, or the weight of uncertainty.
But let's end the night with this: there are children
playing baseball and though the NPR hosts
discussing drones chatter in the background

like white noise, I barely hear it. I watch one child
hit a double, watch dirt rise as he slides,
watch the simplicity of being close to safe
as the thwack of a ball suctions to leather.

America

We ache. We argue against the TV
and our thoughts flatten. We break

a dish in the sink and bleed cleaning it up. We cry
and crawl through crud. We drag and devour

our fate like a feast. We eat
leftovers for breakfast,

evaluate life in therapy. We fumble joy
mid-protest, gamble morals

for morsels. We grasp the grit. We halt,
then humbly ignite. We incite. We jump rope

and recall childhood songs. We jam
our dreams, knit our knots, but still knock

on a neighbor's door. We linger inside
language, then mumble our speech.

We negate. We negotiate
the curve on our bikes. We organize

and open yesterday's mail. We pray, and plummet
in pain, quiz ourselves until we quit. We read,

then rumble our voices louder than tweets.
We stumble, and the sun still rises. We stretch

and topple the takeaway, then unravel.
We uproot what we didn't know was rooted.

We vote and vent with friends. We wait.
We would do more, but how? We x-ray bodies

to find the break's location. We yell
and yearn and zip children's coats

to keep out the cold. We zoom through
an alphabetical list without noticing

our breath that holds us here
. in this chair, without noticing

how small we are
and how small we aren't.

What Remains

Near the edge of Lake Erie, a common tern skims the shoreline
for small fish. Behind me the marsh is golden
with buds of green, migrating warblers flutter their wings
with urgency. I sing a church song he taught me:
"Mountains bow down and seas will roar at the sound

of your name." If waves are mountains, they burst
when they bow to shore. The water is dark blue,
blue like the hallway outside the sanctuary
where he once pulled me to his chest
and I played a game of reaching around the girth
of his body. The hair of his goatee scuffed my neck
and he whispered something. But the speakers crackled
the sermon and then he grew hard between us.

Today, I want to find sand to learn how to burrow.
But I keep noticing the distance between me and the place
where flocks of birds decide this is the day to leave.
I list what I see and know: Lake Erie, song sparrow, pine siskin,
the way a whisper fades across decades. I cling to a stone
before skipping it, watch it bounce across water and sink.

The Dead

So much time is spent erasing.
We cut the onions, the zucchini, mince
garlic and celery, shred carrots and place it all
in a bowl of kale. We eat the food.
What else should we do with all this living?

Tomorrow, I'll watch the sun wander
its same path across the sky. I'll walk
to the post office but forget what I need to mail
or I'll remember and know it's impossible
to write the dead. We ought to have an address
for people who have died. Children drop letters
every December for Santa. It's similar.
But we'd have so many questions ...
Where would the dead leave their answers?

And what of the deaths that have not died?
Those lost friendships, fingernails that knew
so much about growth, the mind with its illness
spinning, that family around the dining room table
with children laughing and bowls being passed one by one.
Where are those bowls and who is doing their passing?

Lake Erie Seiche
for P. C.

The bay of the lake is a fist shoved inland —
our body the body of land — the water a god

who punches the shore in the center
of our chest, leaves a gasp of breath

to name the moment when the inhale
isn't enough. Boulders on the shoreline

behind us are grey and black in their mass,
too heavy to move and sturdy for climbing.

Not falling is our steps' rhythm.
We watch five sailboats drift

with our prayers to know
what comes after my Love and I

say, "I do — " after you and yours
learn to say, "I tried — "

Who told the wind to set, thrust North,
form a seiche on the lake

with no seismic force pushing
the waves, no call from sun or moon?

This lake has no visible course.
We walk the shoreline unsure

what to say, close one eye and cover each boat
with each finger. We push them forward.

Folly Beach: Surf
for E. T.

The first morning of summer eleven pelicans fly
high over water beyond the shoreline.
The sea follows its tide and my surfer
follows the sea, knows there's a present
that passes so quickly it can't be seen
but it can be felt with the ride and push of a board.
He feels the rush of worlds and spins rhythm
on ankle busters. During summer he teaches
beginners like me. I don't know what I'm seeking
or how to catch what I crave, but I turn
my board to shore while behind me
pelicans dive out of hunger, out of necessity.

Memory

The rabbit's tracks grow larger as the snow melts.
So goes memory, I guess. Moments are small:
dancing in the kitchen to the Talking Heads
while I chop what vegetables I have left.

After snow covered the dunes like a shrine,
after waves broke their shape on the shoreline,
after I piled what I could into words, I came home
to tracks and dinner. Who knows what will be

made of this spinach and sweet pepper,
what I'll taste when I finish the dinner
I didn't plan: burnt onions and black beans
heating, potatoes that soften in water.

Outside, tracks in the snow grow larger.
What was seen is no longer as it was.

Genesis VII

Seven are the stars of the big dipper, that shovel
in the sky. What's it digging up there?
Seven never knew the diatonic scale
but it shelled itself to form sound.
There are seven letters in the Roman numeral system.
Count me to sleep or count me to dream.
Seven is the month of fireworks or gunshots,
depends where you are. Seven
never played its luck at craps in Vegas
under the table when the stickman handed the dice
seven face up. Seven could be the mirror
you dropped moving from one apartment
to the next, and the years of bad luck that followed.
Seven are the hours after takeoff, the moment
night begs to be let in, after land shrinks behind a frame
you can study: clouds, a little light, horizon holding
its color tight. Seven could be the big one,
end of the week, God resting, holy day of nothing.

Tender, how

for J. C.

on my way to Kentucky a herd of deer
can't decide which way to move
in the cropped cornfield, statues
under sky, like you in your bleak borough

with the photo of the Ohio river:
how the waves stand on top
of themselves to remind us
nothing is always moving. Tenderness,

how she comes to you, chimes from your chest
a song. Before you let her inside
the alley of you, she whispered, *this is how*
we come into the world, vulnerable and small.

She came to the dog that broke her back
and had to relearn to walk with a slight tail-wag.
She came to the woman after suicide failed
and the bruise of the noose faded to yellow. Tender,

how we notice the white curtains behind us,
swollen streak of sun that cuts through
and wonder how anyone can blame anything
for living the only way it knows how.

Notes

"The Body Keeps the Score" (23) — title taken from, and poem inspired by, Bessel Van der Kolk's book *The Body Keeps the Score: Brain, Mind, and Body in the Healing of Trauma* (Penguin Books, 2014).

"Honored After Rescue Failed" (45) — lifeguard, Dale Laverty, received a Certificate of Commendation in 2016 in Sydney for his attempt to save a man at Fingal Bay in November, 2013. Source: "Award for lifeguard," in the *Port Stephens Examiner,* March 16, 2016.

"The Truth About Love" (57) is inspired by, and responding to, W. H. Auden's poem, "O Tell Me the Truth About Love."

"Mardi Gras in the Bayou" (60) is inspired by Campbell Robertson's article, "Mardi Gras Chase in the Bayou Ends with Gentle Lashings, and Prayers" published in the *New York Times* on February 10, 2016.

Acknowledgements

I would like to thank the editors of the journals where the following poems, sometimes in slightly different versions, first appeared:

Artful Dodge	"Up from the Basement, from the Photo"
CALYX	"Foster Family;" "To the Poet, from the Poem"
Claw & Blossom	"Opossum"
Columbia Journal	"Wing in the Freezer"
Connotation Press	"Body of the Great Blue Heron"
Conte	"Letter to Shame"
The Fourth River	"What Remains," "At the Churchyard"
Great River Review	"Black Swamp Bird Observatory Banding Station;" "Memory;" "Where the goldfinch"
Grist	"Lake Erie Seiche"
Literary Imagination	"Dear Great Blue Heron"
The Louisville Review	"Tender, How;" "The Truth about Love"
Minerva Rising	"Hook & Life;" "Without a Field Guide"
Pittsburgh Poetry Review	"Mardi Gras in the Bayou;" "Because of Beatitude;" "To Clarify;" "Secret"
Parks & Points	"Fieldnotes in February at Dawn"
r.kv.r.y.	"Genesis VII"

Shooter Literary Magazine	"Landscape"
Spillway	"Where Nothing"
Tahoma Literary Review	"Honored After Rescue Failed"
Voyages	"America;" "The Privilege of Watching Neighborhood Baseball;" "What the Bones Say"

I am deeply grateful to the many people who have encouraged, inspired, and challenged me over the years, including Maggie Anderson, Ellen Bass, Jennifer Blatt, Alice Cone, Joey Connelly, Bob Cowser, Jr., Rita Dove, Sarah Dudash, Stephanie Edwards, Anna French, Sarah Friebert, Stuart Friebert, Mark Irwin, Mark Jamison, Dorianne Laux, Edward Micus, Joseph Millar, Robert Miltner, Liz Moore, Carol Neidert, Paul Neidert, Jean Reinhold, Anele Rubin, Amanda Schuster, Ruth Schwartz, Joanna Solfrian, Jim Storad, Richard Tayson, Ellison Thomas, Diane Vreuls, Catherine Wing, and Kathryn Winograd. I am also humbled by and grateful to the land, marshes, and bodies of water, the birds, plants, trees, animals, and insects that helped bring these poems into the world, that kept me in awe of this life, this planet. Thank you to my greyhounds Bill, Betty, Dean, and Cedar for your calm and elegant energy. To Peter Campion, Patrick Davis, and Cory Firestine, thank you for the care and attention you have given to this book. To the Ohio Arts Council and Lilian E. Smith Center, thank you for providing financial support and space. To my partner, Deb Neidert, thank you for standing beside me through it all.

About the Author

Nicole Robinson's poems have appeared in *Columbia Journal,
The Fourth River, Great River Review, The Louisville Review,
Spillway, Tahoma Literary Review,* and elsewhere. She is
the recipient of an Individual Excellence Award for poetry from
the Ohio Arts Council and the Humanities Award from the
American Academy of Hospice and Palliative Medicine. Currently
serving as the narrative medicine coordinator at Akron Children's
Hospital, she resides in Ohio.

About the Type and Paper

Designed by Malou Verlomme of the Monotype Studio, Macklin is an elegant, high-contrast typeface. It has been designed purposely for more emotional appeal.

The concept for Macklin began with research on historical material from Britain and Europe dating to the beginning of the 19th century, specifically the work of Vincent Figgins. Verlomme pays respect to Figgins's work with Macklin, but pushes the family to a more contemporary place.

This book is printed on natural Rolland Enviro Book stock. The paper is 100 percent post-consumer sustainable fiber content and is FSC-certified.

Without a Field Guide was designed by Eleanor Safe and Joe Floresca.

Unbound Edition Press champions honest, original voices. Committed to the power of writers who explore and illuminate the contemporary human condition, we publish collections of poetry, short fiction, and essays. Our publisher and editorial team aim to identify, develop, and defend authors who create thoughtfully challenging work which may not find a home with mainstream publishers. We are guided by a mission to respect and elevate emerging, under-appreciated, and marginalized authors, with a strong commitment to advancing LGBTQ+ and BIPOC voices. We are honored to make meaningful contributions to the literary arts by publishing their work.

unboundedition.com